Wait! W

The BEATLES' Couldn't Read Music?

DAN GUTMAN

illustrated by ALLISON STEINFELD

NORTON YOUNG READERS

An Imprint of W. W. Norton & Company
Celebrating a Century of Independent Publishing

To kids who like to learn cool stuff.

For information about permission to reproduce selections from this book, write to
Permissions, W. W. Norton & Company, Inc., 500 Fifth Avenue, New York, NY 10110

For information about special discounts for bulk purchases, please contact
W. W. Norton Special Sales at specialsales@wwnorton.com or 800-233-4830

Manufacturing by Lake Book Manufacturing
Book design by Hana Anouk Nakamura
Production manager: Delaney Adams

ISBN 978-1-324-05216-6 (cl); 978-1-324-05302-6 (pbk)

W. W. Norton & Company, Inc., 500 Fifth Avenue, New York, N.Y. 10110
www.wwnorton.com

W. W. Norton & Company Ltd., 15 Carlisle Street, London W1D 3BS

1 2 3 4 5 6 7 8 9 0

CONTENTS

Lots of songs and albums are mentioned in this book. Listen to them on records, online, on YouTube, or wherever you get your music.

"Guitar groups are on the way out. The Beatles have no future in show business."

—Decca Records, rejecting the Beatles, 1962

"A guitar's all right, John, but you'll never earn your living by it."

—John Lennon's Aunt Mimi

So May I Introduce
to You . . .

Hi! I'm Turner. This is my sister Paige.

And we are *BeatleMANIACS!*

I know *everything* about the Beatles.

Not as much as me.

Oh yeah? We'll see.

Some kids probably don't even know who the Beatles were. Let me explain. Paul McCartney was a chubby kid. His friend George Harrison had big ears. Their friend John Lennon could barely see, but he wouldn't wear glasses because other kids would think he was a nerd. And Ringo Starr was a sickly, sad-looking kid with a big nose.

These four boys grew up in Liverpool, England, and—with a little help from their friends— became the most famous musical group in history. And here's the amazing thing—none of them could read music.

So what? Irving Berlin couldn't read music.

Who's Irving Berlin?

Are you kidding? He was the most famous songwriter *ever*! He wrote "White Christmas," "There's No Business Like Show Business," "God Bless America"—

Okay, okay! We're not going to tell the *whole* history of the Beatles here. We're going to tell you the cool, *little-known facts* we dug up. Because that's what we do.

Right. For instance, do you know the Beatles song "Ticket to Ride"?

Sure.

Well, Ryde is a town in England. John and Paul went there, and that's what gave them the idea for "Ticket to Ride."

I didn't know that!

3

Neither did I before we started researching this book.

Hey, what's your favorite Beatles song, Paige?

"Good Morning Good Morning"

Same to you. So what's your favorite Beatles song?

"Do You Want to Know a Secret?"

No, I want you to tell me the name of your favorite Beatles song.

"I Will"

Okay, go ahead.

"Tell Me Why"

Because I'm curious!

"Don't Bother Me"

Well, that's rude! Forget I brought it up. Let's just get started with the book.

"When I saw four guys who didn't look like they'd come out of the Hollywood star mill, who played their own songs and instruments . . . I said: 'I know these guys, I can relate to these guys, I am these guys.' This is what I'm going to do—play in a rock band."

—Billy Joel

CHAPTER 1

Stuff Your Teacher Wants You to Know About the Beatles . . .

Most teachers don't really want you to know *anything* about the Beatles! They want you to know about Abraham Lincoln and educational stuff like that. But here's the basic info . . .

July 7, 1940 Ringo Starr is born.

October 9, 1940 John Lennon is born.

June 18, 1942 Paul McCartney is born.

February 25, 1943 George Harrison is born.

July 6, 1957 John and Paul meet.

1960 John, Paul, and George become the Beatles.

1961 They perform at the Cavern Club in
Liverpool.

1962 Brian Epstein becomes their manager.
Ringo joins the group. Their first
record, "Love Me Do," is released.

1963 The first Beatles album comes out. They
have their first number one song,
"Please Please Me." Beatlemania
sweeps England.

1964 They appear on *The Ed Sullivan
Show* in New York. Beatlemania
sweeps America. The movie *A
Hard Day's Night* comes out.

1965 *Rubber Soul* album. *Help!* movie.

1966 *Revolver* album. Their last
concert, in San Francisco.

1967 *Sgt. Pepper's Lonely Hearts Club Band* album. *Magical Mystery Tour* album and movie.

1968 *The White Album. Yellow Submarine* movie.

1969 *Abbey Road* album

1970 *Let It Be* album. The Beatles break up.

Still awake? Okay, let's get to the good stuff . . .

"They blew the walls down for everybody else."
—Barack Obama

CHAPTER 2

So Much Younger Than Today

The Beatles broke up over *fifty* years ago. So why are we still talking about them and listening to their music? There have been *thousands* of rock groups. What was different about these guys?

Lots! When the Beatles started, hardly any singers wrote their own songs or played their own instruments. And back then, groups had a lead singer. The other members of the band were in the background. But the Beatles didn't have a lead singer. They had *four* lead singers.

They also had four personalities. Paul was "the cute one." John was "the clever one." George was "the quiet one." Ringo was "the sad one." So everybody could to relate to one of the Beatles.

But more than anything else, their music was *great*! It sounds as good today as it did when they made it. And no two Beatles songs sound

"I had no idea about doing music as a way of life until rock and roll hit me."
—John Lennon

alike. That's why we remember the Beatles today. They're like Beethoven and Mozart.

Who?

Very funny.

Let's start at the beginning. It all began on July 6, 1957. John Lennon was sixteen. He and his group the Quarry Men were playing at a church fair. It was one of their first shows.

Paul McCartney was fifteen. He rode his bike to the church and a friend introduced him to John, who didn't even know how to tune his guitar. Paul showed him, and he played a few songs. John was impressed, and invited Paul to join the Quarry Men.

Paul went to the Liverpool Institute High School for Boys. He rode the school bus with his friend George Harrison, who was just fourteen.

Not much older than us!

Right, and George also played guitar. In fact, he was better than the other two. He auditioned for John on the upper deck of a bus. At first John didn't want this "little kid" in his band. But when he saw how well George played, he changed his mind and asked him to join the Quarry Men too. Soon they evolved into the Beatles.

And Ringo . . .

We'll get to him later.

Why "Beatles"?

John called his group the Quarry Men because he went to Quarry Bank High School. After he graduated in 1957, the group wanted a new name.

In the 1950s, the word *beat* was in the air. There were "beatniks" and "beat poets." In the 1953 movie *The Wild One* there's a motorcycle gang called "the Beetles."

13

But that's not where they got the name. John, Paul, and George were big fans of Buddy Holly. His backup group was called the Crickets. It made John think of "Beatles."

BEFORE THEY WERE THE BEATLES, they were . . .

✦ Johnny & the Moondogs

✦ Japage 3 (combination of John, Paul, George)

✦ The Nerk Twins (John and Paul)

✦ The Beat Brothers

✦ The Silver Beats

✦ The Silver Beatles

✦ Long John and the Silver Beatles

✦ Big Beat Boppin' Beatles

It's Gotta Be Rock and Roll Music . . .

When the Beatles were teenagers, rock and roll had just been born. Besides Buddy Holly, they loved "Rock Around the Clock" by Bill Haley & His Comets. When Elvis Presley came out with "Heartbreak Hotel" in 1956, John said, "Me whole life changed from then on, I was just completely shaken by it." George heard the song while riding his bike. He said, "What a sound, what a record! It changed the course of my life."

"When you said it, people thought of crawly things, and when you read it, it was beat music."

—John Lennon

That same year Paul bought his first record, "Be-Bop-A-Lula" by Gene Vincent. And when Little Richard released "Long Tall Sally" that year, John said, "It was so great I couldn't speak."

So I guess they spent years taking lessons to become great musicians, right?

Wrong. John had just *one* guitar lesson. He said, "It was so much like school that I gave up." Paul tried taking piano lessons three times. "It seemed boring, like homework," he said.

So how did they get so good?

They taught themselves! And they worked *really* hard. One time, Paul and George heard about a guy in Liverpool who knew how to play a B7 chord on guitar. So you know what they did?

They called him on the phone?

No. They got a map, planned the route, took a bus to the guy's house, and knocked on his door!

Too bad there was no internet in those days.

So they spent years in Liverpool playing at schools, dances, and clubs. They hardly earned any money. And it was a hard life.

Some nights on the road they had to sleep in a freezing van. Paul once said that the only way to stay warm was to lie on top of each other in a "Beatles sandwich." When the guy on top got so cold that hypothermia was setting in, it would be his turn to get on the bottom.

One time, they got a ride on a truck. Paul had to sit on the battery. He was wearing jeans with zippers on the back pockets. Suddenly he jumped up and screamed. The zipper had connected with the positive and negative ends of the battery.

Finally, they were hired to play regularly at a Liverpool jazz club called the Cavern Club. It was a tiny place that had been an air raid shelter during World War II. It stank of cigarettes, hot dogs, and sweat.

On hot days, the walls would be *dripping*. And on cold days, the pounding music made calcium fall from the bricks. The Beatles called it "Liverpool dandruff."

The Cavern was *dangerous*. It was below street level, with only one door in and out. No fire exit. If there had been an emergency, it would have been a disaster.

Then, in 1960, the Beatles were invited to play in Hamburg, West Germany. But there was just one problem.

They didn't have money to get there?

No, they didn't have a drummer.

How could there be a rock group without a drummer?

Well, they had a few drummers, but they didn't have a *regular* drummer. So they found a local guy who had his own drum set, which hardly *anybody* had. His name was Pete Best.

So it was John, Paul, George, and Pete?

Actually, it was John, Paul, George, Pete, and Stu.

Stu? Who's Stu?

He was the bass player. Well, he wasn't very good, but he was John's friend. Anyway, they drove eight hundred miles to Hamburg. It was a rough town, and they played on a street filled with seedy bars.

Often the Beatles had to play eight hours a night. So they had to learn *lots* of songs.

They all lost their voices. It was called getting "Hamburg Throat."

And it was crazy! They would eat onstage, and

19

throw food at each other. Sometimes John would get onstage dressed like a cleaning lady. Or he would perform in his underwear with a toilet seat around his neck. Anything to put on a show.

"He really was a bit loony, in the nicest possible way."
—Paul McCartney

But here's the thing—the Beatles were getting *good*. They made five trips to Hamburg altogether, and spent more than a *thousand* hours onstage there. That's like playing three hours a night for a year. In 1961, they did three hundred and forty shows!

And when they got back to Liverpool, they were the best rock group in town.

Mop Tops

We've got to mention their haircuts. Before the Beatles, boys usually had short hair. Cool guys put grease in their hair and swept it up like Elvis Presley.

"Nobody looked like us. Before not too long, of course, everybody looked like us."

—Paul McCartney

Didn't Julius Caesar have sort of a Beatles haircut?

Well, yeah. But that was a *long* time ago. While the Beatles were in Hamburg, they made friends with three German fans—Klaus, Jurgen, and Astrid. Astrid fell in love with Stu, the bass player. He let her cut his hair just like hers—straight, down, forward, with no grease. Soon after that, John, Paul, and George asked Jurgen to cut their hair the same way. And it became the "Beatles haircut."

After they got famous, men all over the world started wearing their hair longer. It all started with the Beatles.

Brian

The Beatles were getting good and they had cool haircuts, but they weren't famous. When they came home from Germany toward the end of 1961, they almost split up. They weren't making much progress . . . or money.

"I was immediately struck by their music, their beat, and their sense of humor on stage... I knew they would be bigger than Elvis."
—Brian Epstein

And they were all around twenty. That's when there's a lot of pressure on young people to stop fooling around, get a job, and start a career.

That could have been the end of the Beatles right there. But that's when they got a lucky break. It was October 28, 1961. A teenager named Raymond Jones walked into a record store in Liverpool and asked for a record called "My Bonnie." The Beatles had recorded it while they were in Hamburg. They were just the backup group for a singer named Tony Sheridan.

The manager of the record store was Brian Epstein. He was twenty-seven, and his family owned the store. Brian took pride in stocking every new record. The next day, when two girls came in and asked for "My Bonnie," Brian ordered a few copies.

Brian was a natural salesman. When he was sixteen, he worked at his father's furniture store. On his second day of work, a lady came in to buy a mirror, and he sold her a dining room table!

Brian didn't know it, but just two hundred steps from his store the Beatles were playing at the Cavern Club. A few days later, he went to check them out.

Brian had never managed anyone before. But he asked the Beatles if he could be their manager. They said yes, and he got to work.

The first thing he did was give them a makeover. The Beatles mostly wore jeans and leather jackets. Brian knew they wouldn't get on TV or impress a record company dressed like that. So he put them in matching suits and ties.

"If it takes suits to get us on television, and if we need to be on television to be able to promote ourselves, then we will put on suits."
—George Harrison

Brian also had them stop smoking, eating, and clowning around onstage. And he had them end every show with a deep bow to the audience.

One thing Brian *didn't* change was their name. Lots of people said "the Beatles" was a terrible name. But they stuck with it.

Brian was a businessman, and he ran the Beatles like a company. The boys were employees, and every Friday each of them would get a paycheck. In the beginning it was twenty-five pounds, which is about seventy dollars.

That may not sound like much money. But George's father, who was a bus driver, only earned *ten* pounds a week.

The next thing Brian did was try to get the Beatles a record contract. "My Bonnie" wasn't a big seller. They needed to get signed by a major record company.

Decca was one of the biggest ones in England. On January 1, 1962, Brian got an audition with them. The Beatles played fifteen songs. After hearing them, Decca decided that guitar groups were "on the way out."

Ha! That had to be one of the dumbest moves in history!

Other record companies turned down the Beatles too. Things were not looking good. At one gig, they played four hours in front of eighteen people. When it was time to get paid the twenty pounds they were promised, the promoter said he could only pay them twelve.

Ouch! But then they got another break.

Big George

The Beatles had already been turned down by EMI, another big record company. But Brian got a meeting with a producer there named George Martin. He hadn't heard of the Beatles, but he listened to their Decca tape and agreed to have them come in for an audition.

It was June 1962. They drove two hundred miles to London. They were nervous. George Martin was an *important* producer.

The Beatles called him "Mr. Martin" out of respect. Behind his back, they called him "Big George" to avoid confusing him with George Harrison.

"We always referred to George Martin as the grown-up behind the glass window, and we were the kids in the studio."
—Paul McCartney

At that first session, the Beatles played two songs John and Paul had written, "Love Me Do" and "P.S. I Love You."

"I did think they had enormous talent, but it wasn't their music, it was their charisma, the fact that when I was with them they gave me a sense of well-being, of being happy."
—George Martin

When they were done, George Martin said, "if there's anything you don't like, tell me, and we'll try to do something about it." There was silence for a moment, and then George Harrison said, "Well, for a start, I don't like your tie." That broke the ice!

George Martin offered the Beatles a contract to record four more songs. They would only get a penny for every record sold, but they were thrilled. They had a record contract! They were on their way!

There was just one thing George Martin didn't like about the Beatles.

Wait! WHAT? You're gonna end the chapter like that? That's so mean!

Hey, it's called a cliff-hanger, Turner. Deal with it.

CHAPTER 3

Beatlemania

Okay, so what was the one thing George Martin didn't like about the Beatles?

The drummer. He didn't think Pete Best was good enough.

Oh yeah. Actually, the other three had wanted to replace Pete for a while. It wasn't just his drumming. Pete was really shy. He didn't hang out with the others. He didn't have their sense of humor. He didn't get a Beatles haircut. And sometimes he would fall asleep at the drums!

So when George Martin said Pete wasn't good enough, John, Paul, and George decided to replace him.

Ringo Starr was the best drummer in Liverpool. He had played with the Beatles four times on nights when Pete was sick. George Harrison

Love, love me do...

"First hearing 'Love Me Do' on the radio sent me shivery all over. It was the best buzz of all time."
—George Harrison

pushed for Ringo to be invited into the group. And on August 18, 1962, the Beatles played their first show as John, Paul, George, and Ringo.

Those names kind of roll off the tongue, y'know? And it makes sense. John brought in Paul. Paul brought in George. George brought in Ringo.

FYI, Ringo was twenty-two, John was twenty-one, Paul was twenty, and George was nineteen.

Thank you, Mr. Unnecessary Detail! So what happened next?

Some of the fans at the Cavern were angry. They chanted, "Pete forever, Ringo never!" Six days after Ringo replaced Pete, there was a fight at the Cavern. George was hit in the face and got a black eye. The tires on Brian Epstein's car were slashed. But soon the fans got over it and came to accept Ringo.

Poor Pete Best!

Yeah. Two months later, the Beatles' first single "Love Me Do" came out. They were on their way.

Something Was in the Air

Music was changing, the first week in October 1962. In England, the Beatles' first record came out. In California, the first album by the Beach Boys came out. In New York, Bob Dylan had his first big concert.

That's when things started to snowball for the Beatles, at least in England. They made their first TV appearance. "Love Me Do" reached number seventeen on the British pop charts. George Martin said he wanted them to make an album.

In November, they recorded their next single, "Please Please Me." After they finished playing the last note, George Martin pressed the intercom button in the control room and announced, "Gentlemen, you have just made your first number one record."

He was right! In January 1963, "Please Please Me" became number one. Fans started hanging around outside the Beatles' houses. Girls covered their van with love notes and graffiti written in lipstick. The band toured Europe and people went crazy. It was called "Beatlemania."

Yeah, but in the United States, the Beatles were still unknown. Capitol Records, which was owned by EMI, didn't think Americans would like the Beatles' sound. The company didn't release their records here. But then they got *another* lucky break . . .

Let *me* tell it! *The Ed Sullivan Show* was a really popular TV show in the United States. *Everybody* watched it on Sunday nights. Sullivan was at an airport in London when he heard thousands of kids screaming their heads off. He asked what was going on, and was told that it was the Beatles, coming back from a tour in Sweden.

Elvis Presley had been on *The Ed Sullivan Show* in 1956, and he was a sensation. Sullivan arranged for the Beatles to come to America. They appeared on his show on February 9, 1964, and seventy-three *million* people watched. Almost half of the TV sets in America were tuned in.

I heard that crime stopped in America that night. *Everyone* was watching TV.

"The only place we ever got any peace was when we got in the suite and locked ourselves in the bathroom."
—George Harrison

The Beatles conquered America. Every teenager had to own Beatles records, Beatles cards, or a Beatles wig. During one interview George Harrison said he liked jelly beans, and fans began throwing jelly beans at them when the group was onstage.

And the jelly beans in England were *soft*. But the ones in America were hard, like bullets!

What, did you research the history of jelly beans?

Yes! The Beatles were *exploding*! They couldn't step outside without being mobbed. Sometimes Paul would put on a wig and a fake beard so he could sneak out and watch it all happening.

Somebody snuck up behind Ringo and snipped off a lock of his hair for a souvenir.

In Seattle, a hotel tried to make money by cutting up the rugs in the Beatles' rooms and selling the pieces to fans. So do you know what the Beatles did?

> **"**We were driving through Colorado, we had the radio on, and eight of the top ten songs were Beatles songs . . . I knew they were pointing the direction of where music had to go.**"**
>
> —Bob Dylan

They sued the hotel?

No, they peed on the rugs!

Lovely. On April 4, 1964, the top five positions on the Billboard chart were *all* Beatles songs—"Can't Buy Me Love," "Twist and Shout," "She Loves You," "I Want to Hold Your Hand," and "Please Please Me."

Do you think they just got lucky?

I say it was a lot of hard work. In 1963 they did two hundred and fifty-two live shows, thirty-six radio shows, thirty-one TV shows, *and* they recorded two albums. Oh, in the middle of all that, John and his wife Cynthia had a baby.

But they did get some lucky breaks. If any of these hadn't taken place—Brian Epstein, George Martin, Ringo, Ed Sullivan—Beatlemania might not have happened.

It would be a different world.

CHAPTER 4

Let's Talk About John Lennon

John started the Beatles, so he should come first. Like all of them, he had an interesting and tragic life.

John's father, Alfred, worked on ships and was away at sea a lot. He was also in jail a lot. Alf left the family when John was five.

John's mom, Julia, couldn't handle raising a young boy by herself. So her sister Mimi said John could come live with her.

Aunt Mimi rented out rooms of her house. One guest, Harold Phillips, had a harmonica. John was fascinated by it. So Phillips said John could have the harmonica if he could play a tune on it the next morning.

"That was one of the great moments of life, when I got my first harmonica."
—John Lennon

John wasn't interested in sports. He was a bookworm and a class clown. He liked making cartoons, silly stories, and poems. He even created his own newspaper—*Daily Howl*—which he brought to school to make his friends laugh.

During Beatlemania, John published two books of his writing and artwork, *In His Own Write* and *A Spaniard in the Works*.

John had terrible eyesight. He was constantly bumping into things. One time he was over at Paul's house and he went home late at night. The next day, he asked Paul why a group of guys were playing cards on a nearby front lawn at one o'clock in the morning. Paul told him it wasn't a group of guys playing cards. It was a nativity scene!

John finally started wearing glasses because Buddy Holly wore glasses. John's round glasses became so famous they were called "John Lennon glasses."

"He made it okay to wear glasses! I *was* Buddy Holly."
—John Lennon

Aunt Mimi didn't tell John that his mother lived two miles away. But John found out, and when he was fourteen he started visiting Julia. She bought him his first guitar and taught him some banjo chords.

Here's something you probably don't know. Julia used to call John "Stinker" because he made no effort to hide his farts.

Lovely. Anyway, John and the Quarry Men made their first record when he was seventeen. It was July 12, 1958. They went to a little studio where singers could pay a few dollars—I mean *pounds*—to make two songs and take the record home with them. Today, that's one of the most valuable records in the world.

The songs they recorded were Buddy Holly's "That'll Be the Day" and "In Spite of All the Danger," which is the only song credited to "McCartney-Harrison."

Three days after the Quarry Men made that record, John's life was changed forever. His mother was crossing the street when she was hit by a car and killed.

"It was the worst thing that ever happened to me."
—John Lennon

So he lost his mother *twice*?

Yes, and ten years later he wrote the song "Julia" about her.

John had a few jobs before he was famous. He worked in a restaurant, cleaning and waiting on tables. He worked on a construction site with a pickax and shovel. He wanted to earn enough money to buy an electric guitar. But he got fired because he ruined a teapot by putting a flame under it without putting water in it.

John didn't like the sound of his own voice. He would ask George Martin to speed it up, slow it down, or do something to change it. When he sang "Tomorrow Never Knows," John wanted to be hung upside down by a rope and spun around. Instead, they used a rotating speaker.

John met the artist Yoko Ono at a London art gallery in 1966. She had a sculpture that was a piece of wood with nails poking out of it. A sign said you could hammer a nail into the wood, and John asked if he could do that. Yoko said he could hammer in a nail if he paid five shillings. John offered to give her an imaginary five shillings if she'd let him hammer in an imaginary nail. Not long after that, John and his wife Cynthia split up and John married Yoko.

The two of them did nutty stuff like hold a press conference while sitting in a big bag.

But they did serious stuff too. During the Vietnam War, John and Yoko were leaders of the anti-war movement. When they got married in 1969, they spent their honeymoon in a hotel bed with a bunch of friends and recorded the song "Give Peace a Chance."

They moved to New York City in 1971, but President Nixon didn't like John's anti-war statements. He tried to get John kicked out of the United States. So do you know what John did?

Yeah, he announced he had formed a new country called Nutopia! The Nutopian anthem was four seconds of silence. The national flag was a white tissue, and John blew his nose into it.

John died tragically on December 8, 1980. He was killed by a mentally ill Beatles fan in front of John's New York apartment building. He was just forty.

"John Lennon has been my idol all my life."

—Kurt Cobain, of Nirvana

John was not forgotten. Paul and George wrote songs in memory of him, "Here Today" and "All Those Years Ago." And in 2002, the airport in his hometown was renamed Liverpool John Lennon Airport.

After he died, an area in Central Park across from John's apartment was turned into Strawberry Fields, a memorial to John. In the center of it is a mosaic with the title of John's most famous song—IMAGINE.

CHAPTER 5

Let's Talk About Paul McCartney

Okay, do you want to know the most mind-blowing fact about Paul McCartney?

Let's save it for the end of the chapter. That will give readers something to look forward to.

Good thinking. Make 'em wait. What else have you got?

Let's see. When Paul was a kid, his mother, Mary, wanted him to be a doctor. His father, Jim, wanted him to be a scientist. But it was music that Paul loved.

Actually, his father had been bandleader. In the 1920s, he played piano and trumpet in "Jim Mac's Jazz Band." For Paul's birthday one year, his dad gave him a trumpet. But when Paul played it, his lips hurt, so he gave it up.

Also, he realized it's impossible to sing and play trumpet at the same time!

Jim didn't think he was good enough to teach Paul the piano, and he didn't want his son to learn bad habits from him. So Paul taught himself to play.

When he was eleven, Paul cracked his voice on purpose so he'd fail his church choir audition.

Paul and his younger brother Mike shared a bedroom. Their dad wanted the boys to be able to listen to music in bed at night, so he rigged up a radio with wires going up through the living room ceiling to headphones in Paul and Mike's room.

Like with John, Paul's mom died young. Mary McCartney got breast cancer and passed away on Halloween in 1956. She was forty-seven. Paul was just fourteen. That's when he wrote his first song—"I Lost My Little Girl."

Paul wrote "Let It Be" about his mother too. You know, "When I find myself in times of trouble, mother Mary comes to me . . ." He also named his first child Mary.

Like all the Beatles, Paul loved early rockers like Elvis and Little Richard. One of his favorites was Lonnie Donegan, who had a hit with the song "Rock Island Line." After Paul saw Donegan perform, he got permission from his dad to trade in his trumpet for a guitar.

Paul became obsessed with playing guitar. It was his escape after his mom died, and he played all the time.

He liked to play in the bathroom because the sound echoed off the walls in there. His father would shout, "Paul, get off that toilet!"

Eight months after his mother died and three weeks after he turned fifteen, Paul met John. The boys lived a quarter of a mile away from each other. After Paul's dad met John, he said, "He'll get you into trouble, son."

And he did! In those days, teenage boys who wanted to look cool would wear tight jeans. They were called "drainpipe" pants, or "drainies." But Paul's dad and John's aunt Mimi

"It was useless talking to him—I had better conversations with brick walls."

—Paul's brother Mike

didn't approve of drainies. So do you know what the boys did?

They wore two pairs of pants to school?

Yes! On the bus, they would take off one pair and walk into school wearing their drainies.

I read that Paul would have his pants gradually altered so his dad wouldn't notice. He'd leave school at lunchtime and go to a tailor shop. When he came home at the end of the day and his dad complained about the tight pants, Paul would tell him honestly they were the same pants he was wearing that morning.

Before the Beatles got famous, Paul had regular jobs. He delivered newspapers on his bike. He sorted mail at the post office. He was a delivery boy for a department store.

Plenty of people change their name when they go into show business. Paul was afraid "McCartney" might be too long. His real name was James Paul McCartney, and he seriously thought about changing his name to "Paul James."

Actually, his name *was* officially changed in 1997. That's when he was knighted by the queen of England and became "Sir Paul McCartney."

Because John was right-handed and Paul was a lefty, they could sit face-to-face while they were playing guitar and writing songs together, and they could share a microphone more easily when they were performing.

Paul's favorite Beatles song was "Here, There and Everywhere."

In 1966, Paul fell off a moped and cut his lip. He grew a mustache to cover it up, and then the rest of the Beatles grew mustaches too.

Paul asked the writer Isaac Asimov to help him develop a science fiction movie about aliens from another planet who impersonate a rock band.

In 1975 Paul was eating a meal of lamb when he saw some lambs in a field. He became a vegetarian. His voice is in an episode of *The Simpsons* titled "Lisa the Vegetarian."

He loved animals, and kept rabbits, ducks, chickens, dogs, and other furry friends on his property.

One night he left his car window open, and the chickens got in and wrecked it.

Paul was at JFK Airport and witnessed the 9/11 attack on New York. Afterward, he helped organize the Concert for New York City, and released a song called "Freedom." He also performed at the big charity events, such as Live Aid and Band Aid.

He never seemed to stop working. After the Beatles split up, he recorded songs with Stevie Wonder, Michael Jackson, Kanye West, Rihanna, and his own band Wings.

He performed the halftime show at the 2005 Super Bowl, and the opening ceremonies at the 2012 Summer Olympics in London.

And he had a small part in the movie *Pirates of the Caribbean: Dead Men Tell No Tales*.

He also wrote poetry, painted, and wrote four children's books!

Y'know, we can't talk about Paul McCartney without mentioning the "Paul is dead" rumor.

Oh yeah. It started in 1967 and blew up two years later when a Detroit DJ mentioned it on the radio. The rumor was that Paul died in a car crash and a look-alike took his place.

There was no internet back then. But the story spread like crazy. People began searching for clues in Beatles songs and on their album covers.

✦ At the end of "Strawberry Fields Forever" John says, "I buried Paul." (He always insisted it was "cranberry sauce.")

✦ On the cover of *Sgt. Pepper's Lonely Hearts Club Band* there's a hand over Paul's head, which is a symbol of death. And inside the cover is a picture of Paul with an "OPD" arm patch. Officially Pronounced Dead? (It was actually Ontario Police Department.)

✦ In "Glass Onion," John sings "The walrus was Paul." In Scandinavia, the walrus is a symbol of death.

✦ On the cover of *Abbey Road*, the Beatles are walking across the street. It looks like a funeral procession—John is dressed like a priest, Ringo is the mortician, George is the gravedigger, and Paul is the deceased.

✦ In the background of that picture is a Volkswagen Beetle (get it?) with the license plate "28IF." Paul would have been twenty-eight years old . . . *if he had lived!* (Actually, he was still only twenty-seven.)

There are lots of other silly clues. Meanwhile, the whole time, Paul was living happily on his farm in Scotland.

It was the biggest hoax in rock history. Paul made fun of it himself. In 1993 he released a concert album titled *Paul Is Live!*

"Do I look dead? I'm as fit as a fiddle."

—Paul McCartney

R.I.P. PAUL McCARTNEY

"We weren't able to read music or write it down, so we just made it up."
—Paul McCartney

Okay, are you ready for the most mind-blowing fact about Paul McCartney?

Hit me.

Okay, here it is—Paul had hairy legs.

That's *it*?

No, there's more. Not only did he have hairy legs, but he liked to have his legs *combed*.

Wait. WHAT?

It's true! As a teenager, he had a girlfriend

named Iris. Paul would go over her house and Iris's mother would comb his leg hair.

No way! You made that up!

I did not! Iris said, "Paul used to like her combing his legs. He had really hairy legs and he'd come in from the Cavern all tired, roll up his trousers, and she used to comb his legs."

Okay, that's just weird.

CHAPTER 6

Let's Talk About George Harrison

 Okay, what do you have on George?

 Plenty! He was named after King George. His

father said, "If it's good enough for the King it should be good enough for him."

Before he discovered music, George liked playing soccer and cricket.

He was a mischievous kid. George once asked a friend's parent to sign his report card so his own parents wouldn't see it.

One time, George was doing something naughty at school and his teacher hit him with a ruler. He meant to hit George's hand, but it got him on the wrist and left a nasty bruise. The next day his dad came to school, pulled the teacher out of class, and punched him in the nose!

When George was twelve, he saw the country singer Slim Whitman on TV. George had never even *seen* a guitar before. But he decided he had to have one. His mother got him a cheap used guitar, but it didn't last.

Why not?

George wondered what would happen if he unscrewed a bolt in the guitar's neck. The neck fell off and he couldn't get it back on.

Slim Whitman also inspired Paul. Both of them were lefties, but Paul had learned to play guitar right-handed because that's the way everybody else played. Then Paul saw a photo of Slim Whitman playing left-handed. Paul unwound the strings, put them back in reverse order, and started playing lefty.

Hey, this chapter isn't about Paul. Focus!

Okay! Like the other Beatles, George loved rock and roll. He drew pictures of guitars in his schoolbooks instead of paying attention to the teacher.

Besides guitars, George loved cars, and he was

the first Beatle to buy one. He watched the British Grand Prix as a kid and was such a fan that he wrote to his favorite drivers asking for autographs. Later in life, he wrote a song about racing called "Faster."

And, like the others, young George had regular jobs. He rode his bike to deliver meat for a butcher, and he was an apprentice electrician in a department store.

George was called "the quiet Beatle" when the group first toured America. That was partly because he had strep throat, and doctors told him not to talk too much.

When the Beatles were filming a scene in the movie *Help!*, there were some Indian musicians in a restaurant. George saw the sitar—a stringed instrument—and learned how to play it. You can hear it on "Norwegian Wood" and "Within You Without You."

Actually, that wasn't the first time George heard Indian music. His mother, Louise, played it while she was pregnant with George. She felt the gentle music would bring peace and calm to her baby.

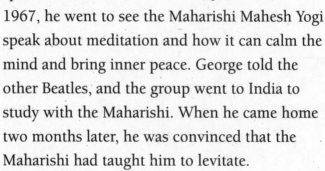

I think it worked. George was the most spiritual Beatle. In 1967, he went to see the Maharishi Mahesh Yogi speak about meditation and how it can calm the mind and bring inner peace. George told the other Beatles, and the group went to India to study with the Maharishi. When he came home two months later, he was convinced that the Maharishi had taught him to levitate.

John and Paul wrote nearly all the Beatles' songs, but some of that talent rubbed off on George. As an exercise to see if he could write a song, he wrote "Don't Bother Me." It's on the album titled *With the Beatles*.

George kept getting better as a songwriter, and went on to write three of the Beatles' most famous songs—"Something," "While My Guitar Gently Weeps," and "Here Comes the Sun."

"Something" has been recorded by over a hundred and fifty singers, including Elvis, Frank Sinatra, and Ray Charles. Sinatra called it "one of the best love songs I believe to be written in fifty or one hundred years."

But George's biggest hit was "My Sweet Lord," which came out after the Beatles split up. He got sued for that one, because the tune is the same as the song "He's So Fine" by the Chiffons. George lost the case and had to pay over a quarter of a million dollars.

George had a good sense of humor. While they were in Germany, the Beatles used to get letters from fans back home. One girl offered to wash George's car for him. As a prank, he told her to take the dirty water over to Paul's house and dump it on his car.

Also, he dedicated his autobiography "to gardeners everywhere."

Tragedy found all the Beatles at some point. In 1997, George got throat cancer. He survived that, but two years later he became the second Beatle to be attacked by a mentally ill person. A man broke into George's house while he and his wife were sleeping and attacked both of them with a kitchen knife. George had a punctured lung.

He survived that too. But in 2001, George was diagnosed with a brain tumor. There was no treatment. To avoid the press, Paul invited George to spend his final days at a house he owned in California. That's where George died on November 29, 2001. He was fifty-eight.

After George's death, a pine tree was planted in his memory. Sadly, the tree didn't last very long. Do you want to know why?

There was a beetle infestation?

Yes! Gee, I hate to end this chapter on a sad note. Do you have one more George story?

Yeah! One day, George's son Dhani was chased home from school and teased by kids singing "Yellow Submarine." Dhani didn't understand why they did that. After he figured it out, he confronted his dad.

"Why didn't you tell me you were in the Beatles?" he asked.

"Oh, sorry," George replied. "Probably should have told you that."

"I think we gave hope to the Beatles fans. We gave them a positive feeling that there was a sunny day ahead."
—George Harrison

CHAPTER 7

Let's Talk About Ringo Starr

First things first. We should explain how he got his name.

Right. His real name was Richard Starkey. Johnny Ringo was an American outlaw. There have been movies about him, like *Gunfight at the O.K. Corral*. Also, there's a character named "The Ringo Kid" in the movie *Stagecoach*.

For his sixteenth birthday, his mother gave him a ring. He liked it, and he got himself another one . . . and another one. Once he got to three rings, people started calling him Ringo.

When he was asked why he wore so many rings, he replied, "I wear them on my fingers because I can't fit them through my nose."

And Starr? When Ringo was growing up in the 1950s, the American singer Kay Starr was popular in England. But Ringo probably changed his last name to "Starr" because it was short for "Starkey," and it sounded good as a stage name.

"I cut the name in half and added an 'r.'"
—Ringo Starr

Okay, enough about the name. Ringo was the oldest Beatle. He was born three months before John.

And he was the poorest Beatle. He grew up in Dingle, a tough neighborhood in Liverpool. The other Beatles sometimes called him "Dingle Boy." His house had a toilet in the yard.

Ringo's first childhood memory was of being pushed in his baby carriage while he was being chased by a goat. That's weird!

When Ringo was a kid, he came up with an idea to get rich—he was going to write letters to wealthy people like Frank Sinatra and ask them to lend him a million dollars.

But seriously, Ringo had a *really* hard childhood. His father left after Ringo's third birthday. His mother, Elsie, scraped together a living by cleaning houses.

When he was six, Ringo got sick. His appendix burst, which led to peritonitis. He fell into a coma. The doctors told his mother three times that Ringo probably wouldn't survive the night.

He was barely conscious for sixteen weeks. He turned seven while he was in a coma.

That's not the end of it. In the hospital, Ringo wasn't allowed out of bed while he was recovering from surgery. He got a toy bus as a gift, and wanted to show it to the boy in the next bed. As he leaned over, Ringo fell out of bed. That ripped his stitches open. He had to stay in the hospital another six months.

At that point, he hadn't learned to read or write. His babysitter taught him when he was nine.

That's not the end of Ringo's problems. When he turned fourteen, he got sick *again*. This time it was pleurisy and tuberculosis. He had to spend another ten weeks in the hospital. Altogether, he spent two years of his childhood in hospitals.

When he finally got out, he had fallen so far behind that there was no point in going back to school. So he left. The weird thing is that after he was famous, the school made money by charging people to sit at Ringo's old desk.

But two good things came out of all that time he spent in hospitals. He learned how to drum, and he learned how to knit.

Knit?

Yeah. Lying in a hospital bed is boring. So he tried knitting.

The nice thing was, a music teacher came to the hospital with instruments for the kids to play. Ringo would only join the hospital band if he could play a drum.

When he was growing up, Ringo's grandparents gave him a mandolin, a banjo, and a harmonica.

He wasn't interested. But he loved keeping a beat. He was always banging on the backs of chairs or tapping coconut shells together.

 Ringo's first drum was homemade. He attached a wire across a biscuit tin. After that, he bought a used bass drum. Then his stepfather got him a used drum kit. It had a cymbal made from a garbage can lid.

"That's where I really started playing. I never wanted anything else from there on."
—Ringo Starr

People say Ringo's drumming sounds different from other drummers'.

Do you think that's because he was left-handed?

No, I think it's because his grandmother forced him to use his right hand instead of his left.

Why?

She believed lefties were possessed by witches, or the devil.

Wait. WHAT?

In those days many people thought there was something wrong with lefties, and they needed to be converted.

That's weird!

Okay, done with the childhood stuff?

That's all I've got.

When he was eighteen, Ringo had a gray streak in his hair. It was probably because of everything he'd been through as a kid.

Like the other Beatles, Ringo had regular jobs. He was a railroad messenger boy, a waiter on a steamship, a woodworking apprentice . . .

He wanted to become a hairdresser, and open his own salon. But drumming led him to the Liverpool music scene. He played with a popular band called Rory Storm and the Hurricanes.

Ringo had a beard back then. When he was invited to join the Beatles, John told him to shave it off so they would all look the same.

In the beginning, he didn't talk much when the Beatles had press conferences. He had just joined the band and he didn't feel he should be the center of attention. Also, he looked a little sad and moody, so the press described him that way. "I'm quite happy inside," he said, "it's just the face won't smile."

During Beatlemania other singers sang songs about Ringo, like "I Want to Kiss Ringo Goodbye" and "Ringo for President."

My favorite was "Ringo, I Love You." The singer's name was Bonnie Jo Mason. Later she became famous under another name—Cher. That was her first record!

Ringo wasn't a *great* singer, but he had a nice voice. John and Paul usually wrote a song for him on each album. You've probably heard him sing "Yellow Submarine" and "With a Little Help from My Friends." He also sang the lead on "I Wanna Be Your Man," "Boys," "Matchbox," "Honey Don't," "Act Naturally," "Good Night," and "What Goes On."

He wasn't known as a songwriter either, but he wrote and sang two Beatles songs, "Don't Pass Me By" and "Octopus's Garden."

Actually, he wouldn't eat octopus, but he was on a boat one time when it was served. The captain told him all about octopuses, and that's what inspired the song.

Ringo also inspired songs written by John and Paul. He would say odd things that sort of made sense. The Beatles called them "Ringo-isms." Like, one day out of the blue he said "Tomorrow Never Knows." The next thing he knew, that became a Beatles song.

One time after a concert, the Beatles were sitting around relaxing and Ringo came out with, "It's been a hard day's night." John rushed to write the song and it became the title of the Beatles' first movie.

When he was twenty-four, Ringo got sick *again*.

Oh no!

He was a Beatle then, and a TV newscaster announced that Ringo had his toenails removed.

Wait. WHAT?

Actually, it was a mistake. Ringo had his *tonsils* removed! But even so, he had tonsillitis and had to go to the hospital. It was during the height of Beatlemania. The group was in the middle of a tour, and they didn't want to cancel concerts and disappoint thousands of fans. So they hired a drummer named Jimmy Nicol to take Ringo's place. He even got a Beatles haircut. Jimmy Nicol played eight concerts, and then Ringo came back.

What ever happened to that guy?

He formed a band called Jimmy Nicol & the Shubdubs.

Shubdubs?

It's for real! He was a Shubdub. But for one glorious week, Jimmy Nicol was a Beatle.

Ringo loved country music, cowboy movies, and photography. He was billed as the director of photography on *Magical Mystery Tour* and published a book of his photos in 2015.

He was not only a musician and photographer. Ringo was also a successful actor. After starring in the Beatles movies *A Hard Day's Night* and *Help!,* he acted in *The Magic Christian, Candy,* and other movies.

Well, that made sense. Remember the Beatles song "Act Naturally"? Ringo sang, "They're gonna put me in the movies. They're gonna make a big star out of me."

He was a TV star too. In the 1980s, Ringo was on the series "Princess Daisy," and he played Mr. Conductor on the kids' show *Shining Time Station.*

And he was in an episode of *The Simpsons*, "Brush with Greatness."

When he was acting in the movie *Caveman*, he met actress Barbara Bach. They got married in 1981. And here's a little-known fact—Barbara's sister Marjorie married Joe Walsh, a guitarist with the Eagles. So that means that Ringo and Joe Walsh are brothers-in-law.

Believe it or not, in 1979 Ringo almost died *again*. He had stomach problems, and part of his intestines were removed.

Man, that guy couldn't catch a break!

Well, he caught one in 2017. Ringo was knighted and he became "Sir Ringo Starr." Not bad for a poor, funny-looking guy with a big nose who barely survived childhood.

"I've come to terms with my nose. It's the talking point when people discuss me. I have to laugh—it goes up one nostril and out the other."

—Ringo Starr

CHAPTER 8

The Songs

The Beatles recorded over two hundred songs. Hey, Paige, let's take turns and say something most people don't know about a Beatles song. You start.

Okay. "Yellow Submarine." The nickname of the Spanish soccer team Villarreal is the Yellow Submarine, and their fans sing the song during games.

"Hey Jude." When Paul started singing, Ringo was in the bathroom. He came running into the studio and tiptoed over to his drum kit just in time to play his part.

"All You Need Is Love." As it fades out, you can hear somebody sing, "She loves you, yeah, yeah, yeah."

"It Won't Be Long." They sing the word "yeah" fifty-five times. That's one "yeah" every 2.4 seconds!

"Good Morning Good Morning." John was inspired by a TV commercial for cornflakes.

"Blackbird." This was about the civil rights movement. Paul wrote it a few weeks after Martin Luther King was killed.

"Sun King." In this song John sings some words that seem to be in Spanish. But he just made up words that *sound* Spanish.

"When I'm Sixty-Four." Paul wrote the music

when he was sixteen. He wrote the lyrics eight years later, to honor his father's sixty-fourth birthday.

 "While My Guitar Gently Weeps." George decided to open a book randomly and write a song based on the first words he saw. They were "gently weeps."

"I always like people doing my songs. It's a great compliment."

—Paul McCartney

"Yesterday"

MTV and *Rolling Stone* magazine named it the best pop song *ever*. So I need to talk about it more. "Yesterday" has been recorded by over two *thousand* singers, from Elvis to Frank Sinatra.

Paul was just twenty-two when he wrote it. He woke up in the middle of the night with the tune in his head. He thought he might have heard it before. So he asked people if they knew it, and they all said it was original.

When he was working on the words, Paul's title was "Scrambled Eggs."

This was the first time a Beatle recorded a song without any of the others. Paul also recorded "Mother Nature's Son" by himself.

"Julia." This was the one song John recorded by himself. And George was the only Beatle playing on "Within You Without You."

None of the Beatles played an instrument on "She's Leaving Home," "Good Night," or "The Inner Light."

"Do You Want to Know a Secret?" Boy bands used to be afraid they'd lose female fans if word got out that one of the boys was married. John married Cynthia Powell in 1962 and then he wrote "Do You Want to Know a Secret?" He even had George sing it so people wouldn't guess the true meaning.

John based it on the song "I'm Wishing" from the Disney film *Snow White and the Seven Dwarfs*, which had the words, "Wanna know a secret? Promise not to tell?"

"Eleanor Rigby." When he was a kid, Paul would visit an old lady who lived alone and he helped her with her shopping. Years later, she inspired this song. The name "Eleanor Rigby" is carved on a tombstone in the churchyard where John and Paul met. But Paul said the original name for the song was "Daisy Hawkins."

If You Listen Carefully . . .

 You'll hear secret messages the Beatles hid in their songs . . .

✦ "Paperback Writer." In the background, John and George sing the French nursery rhyme "Frère Jacques."

✦ "I'm Only Sleeping." At two minutes and one second into the song, somebody yawns.

✦ "Good Morning Good Morning." At the end there are a bunch of animal sounds—a rooster, a cat, a dog, and a lion. John put those sounds in order so each animal would be able to eat the one that came before it.

✦ Speaking of animals, here's an Easter egg no human has heard. At the end of *Sgt. Pepper*, the Beatles put in a twenty-thousand-hertz frequency tone. Humans can't hear it, but dogs can. Paul said, "Why just make records for humans?"

uh oh.

"Eight Days a Week." Paul liked to drive fast, and his driver's license was taken away in 1963. So he hired a driver to take him to John's house for a writing session. On the way there, Paul asked the driver how he was doing, and the driver replied, "I've been working eight days a week." Paul ran into John's house and said, "Got the title."

"Golden Slumbers." The words are based on a four-hundred-year-old poem.

"Lucy in the Sky with Diamonds." John's son Julian came home from school with a picture he made of Lucy O'Donnell, the girl who sat next to him. John asked what the title was, and Julian said, "Lucy in the Sky with Diamonds."

"A Day In the Life." At the end, forty-two musicians in an orchestra were told to play the lowest note on their instrument and gradually move up to the highest note. For the last note, every piano in the building was brought into the studio, and an E chord was played on all of them at the same time. The chord hangs in the air for over forty seconds.

"She Came in Through the Bathroom Window." A fan actually climbed into Paul's bathroom window. Fans would often break into his home and take things as souvenirs. Even his toilet paper! And speaking of toilet paper, to make the sound effects for "Lovely Rita," they played metal combs with toilet paper on them.

Hmmm, it's interesting how so many of your songs involve toilets.

Just a coincidence! "Long Tall Sally" was the first song Paul sang in public, at summer camp. He was fifteen. It was also the *last* song the Beatles sang in concert.

"Martha My Dear." This song was about Paul's dog.

"The Continuing Story of Bungalow Bill." John's wife Yoko and Ringo's first wife, Maureen, are two of the background voices.

"Across the Universe." The background voices are two fans who hung around outside the Beatles' studio. In 2008, this song was beamed into space to celebrate the fiftieth anniversary of NASA and the fiftieth anniversary of the Beatles.

"Because." This song was inspired by the chords from Beethoven's "Moonlight Sonata" played in reverse order.

"All My Loving." This is the only song in which Paul wrote the words first and the music later.

"Revolution #9." This is the longest Beatles track—eight minutes and fifteen seconds. And "Her Majesty" is the shortest—twenty-three seconds.

"Everybody's Got Something to Hide Except Me and My Monkey." This is the longest *title* of a Beatles song.

"I Feel Fine." John leaned his guitar against an amplifier, which made a loud feedback buzz. The Beatles thought it sounded cool, so they kept it in and used it to start the song. It was one of the first times anyone put feedback on record.

Mostly, the Beatles wrote their own songs. But when they were starting out they recorded songs written by other people, like Chuck Berry ("Roll Over Beethoven"), Carole King ("Chains"), Buddy Holly ("Words of Love"), Little Richard ("Long Tall Sally"), Smokey Robinson ("You've Really Got a Hold on Me"), and Burt Bacharach ("Baby It's You").

"I just loved the idea of kids singing it."
—Paul McCartney, about "Yellow Submarine"

The Beatles made songs for kids, like "Ob-La-Di, Ob-La-Da," "All Together Now," "Yellow Submarine," and "Octopus's Garden." For those last two, they blew bubbles through straws to make the sound effects.

When they recorded a song, the Beatles would sing it over and over again until they were happy with the result.

"We worked like dogs to get it right." —Ringo Starr

There were forty-seven takes of "Ob-La-Di, Ob-La-Da." After spending forty-two hours working on it, John came to hate the song. They did "I Will" sixty-seven times. They did *a hundred and one* takes of George's "Not Guilty." And that song never even appeared on a Beatles album! George put it on one of his solo albums.

"Whenever a Beatles song comes on the radio, I reach for the volume and turn it up, because I still haven't gotten enough of them."
—Jerry Seinfeld, comedian

Lucy in the sky

CHAPTER 9

The Albums

The Beatles recorded their first album on February 11, 1963.

Are you saying they did the whole album *in one day*? I thought it took weeks, or months!

It usually does. But they started at ten in the morning and finished before midnight. They saved "Twist and Shout" for last because it was a real screamer. They were afraid John would ruin his voice if he sang that song earlier. When you listen to it, you can hear him straining.

"My voice wasn't the same for a long time after; every time I swallowed, it was like sandpaper."

—John Lennon

They were going to call that first album *Off the Beatle Track*, but decided to go with *Please Please Me* instead.

And they were going to shoot the cover at the insect house of the London Zoo—beetles, get it? But the Zoological Society of London said no.

Their second album—*With the Beatles*—was released on November 22, 1963, the same day John F. Kennedy was killed. Ten weeks later, Beatlemania came to America. It's been said the Beatles helped America heal after the tragedy of losing the president.

At first John and Paul wrote short, simple songs. Y'know, "Love Me Do." "She Loves You." Stuff like that. On their first album, no song was three minutes long, and three of them were under *two* minutes. But soon they were writing more complicated songs, like "Norwegian Wood" and "Nowhere Man." After recording that first album in a day, they spent a month working on *Rubber Soul* and more than *two* months on *Revolver*.

We Hope You Will Enjoy the Show

And then came *Sgt. Pepper's Lonely Hearts Club Band*. They worked on it for almost *five* months. Seven hundred hours!

By 1966, the Beatles' music had become too complicated to perform in concert. So they decided to stop touring and just make music in the studio.

They were sick of Beatlemania anyway. All those screaming fans couldn't hear the music, and neither could the Beatles.

Paul had the idea for the Beatles to pretend to be *another* band and record an album as if they were somebody else.

There was talk of calling the album *Dr. Pepper* until somebody realized a soda company owned the rights.

I heard that Paul was having dinner with the Beatles' roadie Mal Evans. Mal asked, "Will you pass the pepper?" Paul didn't hear him and said, "What? Sergeant Pepper?" That's where the name came from.

❝ *Sgt. Pepper's Lonely Hearts Club Band* is probably the greatest single album I ever heard. ❞

—Brian Wilson, of the Beach Boys

Three days after *Sgt. Pepper* came out, Jimi Hendrix performed the title song in London, with George and Paul in the audience.

For the cover of the album, Brian Epstein wanted a plain brown paper bag. But the Beatles decided to go all-out. They wore marching band uniforms and surrounded themselves with photos of their heroes—Marilyn Monroe, Marlon Brando, Oscar Wilde, Edgar Allan Poe, Lenny Bruce, Albert Einstein . . .

Hey, we wrote about him in *Albert Einstein Was a Dope?*

Right! A year later, the Beatles released another album, and this one had *nothing* on the cover. No photo. No drawing. It was just white. So it was called *The White Album.*

Sometimes simple is best. It was like that with the *Abbey Road* album too. Their first idea was to call it *Everest*. The Beatles were going to fly to Nepal and shoot the cover in front of Mount Everest.

"I wasn't a Beatles fan until I listened to *The White Album* and became an instant convert."

—Steven Spielberg

What a hassle.

So, instead, they just went outside the recording studio on Abbey Road and had the picture taken as they walked across the street. It took ten minutes.

And today, Abbey Road is the most famous street in London. Every tourist has a picture taken of themselves crossing the street.

Random Facts About
Beatles Albums . . .

Rubber Soul was the first one that doesn't have the band's name on the cover.

The *Rubber Soul* cover photo looks stretched-out. When the photographer was showing it to the Beatles, he projected it on a piece of cardboard. It fell backward and the image was distorted. Everybody thought it looked cool, so they used it.

The cover of *Revolver* was designed by Klaus Voorman, their old friend from Hamburg. He was also a bass player, and he appeared on albums by John, George, and Ringo.

John once bought a suit of armor and named it "Sidney." You can see a tiny photo of him wearing it on the cover of *Revolver*.

For the cover of *Yesterday and Today*, somebody got the bright idea of having the Beatles wear bloodstained smocks while holding pieces of raw meat and plastic dolls with no heads. Seventy-five thousand copies were printed before anybody realized the cover might be offensive.

"I thought it was gross."
—George Harrison

Gee, ya think?

A picture of the Beatles sitting around a big trunk was pasted over the covers. The original "butcher cover" became a valuable collector's item.

The early Beatles albums in England had fourteen songs on them. The ones released in

America only had twelve. So there are compilation albums that were only released in America with the leftover songs.

John and Yoko were inseparable. When Yoko got hurt in a car accident, John had a bed brought into the recording studio for her. While the Beatles were making *Abbey Road*, Yoko was lying in the bed, or under the piano on a mattress.

I'd try another take.

At the end of *Sgt. Pepper*, there are a few seconds of gibberish. The Beatles spent a whole night creating that noise, almost as long as it took them to record their first album.

CHAPTER 10

The Impact of
the Beatles

The Beatles changed everything—music,
hairstyles, fashion, attitudes.

It's like they did everything before anybody else.
They were the first rock group to write their
own songs and play their own instruments.
They were the first to do stadium concerts . . .

They were the first to begin a song with a fade in—"Eight Days a Week." And the first major rock group to use a sitar—"Norwegian Wood" . . .

The first to print lyrics on an album cover—*Sgt. Pepper.* And John was the first rock star to write a book . . .

They were first to appear on a live, worldwide satellite TV program. Four hundred million people watched them sing "All You Need Is Love" . . .

The first to record music *backward.* When they finished the song "Rain," John brought the tape home and accidentally put it on his tape player backward. It sounded cool, so they decided to keep it as part of the song. They also used backward music in "Strawberry Fields Forever" and "I'm Only Sleeping."

The point is, the Beatles started a revolution, and not just by singing "Revolution." They inspired thousands of other musicians. After the Beatles broke through, lots of other British bands became famous—the Rolling Stones, the Who, the Kinks, the Animals, and others. It was called "the British Invasion."

Sting was at a swimming pool when he heard "Love Me Do" for the first time. That was when he decided to devote his life to music.

Jimmy Page of Led Zeppelin said, "If it hadn't been for the Beatles, there wouldn't be anyone like us around."

Elvis Costello was in a Beatles fan club when he was eleven.

Americans were inspired too. Kurt Cobain wrote his first song after listening to *Meet the Beatles* in his bedroom.

Teddy Pendergrass was inspired to become a singer after hearing "I Want to Hold Your Hand."

The first song Aerosmith recorded was the Beatles song "I'm Down."

"The minute I saw the Beatles on *The Ed Sullivan Show* — and it's true of thousands of guys — there was the way out. I really saw in the Beatles that here's something I could do. I knew I could do it. It wasn't long before there were groups springing up in garages all over the place."

—Tom Petty

In Canada, Neil Young got up in his high school cafeteria and sang the Beatles' "It Won't Be Long." It was the first time he performed for an audience.

Post Malone has tattoos of John and George on his fingers!

Not everybody liked the Beatles. A review in *Newsweek* said, "Musically, they are a near-disaster." Noël Coward, the British playwright, said, "They are totally devoid of talent."

106

When the Beatles came to America, the author William F. Buckley wrote a newspaper article with the headline "Yeah, Yeah, Yeah, They Stink!"

He said, "The Beatles are not merely awful. They are so unbelievably horrible."

But, love 'em or hate 'em, the Beatles inspired all kinds of people. Rappers like Lil Wayne, Wu-Tang Clan, Frank Ocean, Run-DMC, and the Beastie Boys mentioned the Beatles in their music.

"You can't love music without loving the Beatles."
—Nick Cannon

Comedians . . .

> **"Growing up, I liked all the stuff that everyone else was listening to, like Motown, but the biggest group of all was the Beatles."**
>
> —Eddie Murphy

Talk show hosts . . .

> **"When I was . . . on welfare, the only decoration in a room I shared with a half brother and sister were Beatles posters."**
>
> —Oprah Winfrey

Business leaders . . .

"My model for business is the Beatles. They were four guys who kept each other's negative tendencies in check. They balanced each other and the total was greater than the sum of the parts. And that's how I see business. Great things in business are never done by one person, they are done by a team of people."

—Steve Jobs

You could even say the Beatles changed history. They're the reason the Soviet Union collapsed.

Wait! WHAT? Get outta here! "Back in the U.S.S.R." is all about how great Russia was.

Yeah, but Russians weren't allowed to hear it! Beatles music was banned in the Soviet Union.

The government called it evil. Kids were thrown out of school for playing Beatles records. But Russian kids found a way to get them. The Beatles represented freedom and fun. Russian kids figured maybe the West wasn't as bad as they'd been told. Maybe their leaders had been lying to them. And the Soviet Union collapsed.

Yeah, but you can't say the Beatles made that happen.

I don't have to . . .

"More than any ideology, more than any religion, more than Vietnam or any war or nuclear bomb, the single most important reason for the diffusion of the Cold War was . . . the Beatles."

—Mikhail Gorbachev, former president of the Soviet Union

CHAPTER 11

And in the End . . .

It's hard to believe the Beatles were only together for twelve years, and they were only *famous* for six. When they broke up in 1970, none of them were thirty years old.

They nearly broke up before that. George quit for a week while they were working on *Let It Be*. Ringo walked out while they were making *The White Album*.

We should talk about what finally broke up the Beatles.

There are entire books on the subject. There were business reasons, personal problems, and musical differences. But basically, I think they simply grew up. These four people started out together as boys and became very famous men. Twelve years is a long time for a group of guys to stick together.

"People keep talking about it as if it's the end of the earth. It's only a rock group that split up."
—John Lennon

Standing Solo in the Sun

All the Beatles had successful solo careers. John and Paul both started new bands with their wives, Yoko and Linda.

John's most famous song—"Imagine"—came after the Beatles broke up. Who knows what he might have accomplished if he hadn't died young?

Same with George. After years of being overshadowed by John and Paul, he had a huge success in 1970 with his triple album *All Things Must Pass*. The next year he had another triple album, *The Concert for Bangladesh*. It was the first big charity rock concert.

In the eighties, George teamed up with Bob Dylan, Tom Petty, Jeff Lynne, and Roy Orbison to form the Traveling Wilburys. Do you know how they got that name?

No clue.

George was working on an album and whenever there was a mistake, he'd say, "We'll bury it in the mix." Get it? Wilbury? We'll bury?

I get it. And people often rank Ringo as the least-talented member of the group. But when the Beatles broke up, he was the one pumping out hits like "It Don't Come Easy," "You're Sixteen," and "Photograph."

Ringo and Paul were still making music and selling out concerts in their eighties. Paul's 2020 album *McCartney III* made him the first artist to have a new album in the top two chart positions in each of *six* decades! He was rock's first billionaire.

Paul loved to collect stuff from other celebrities. He bought the bass that was used on Elvis's "Heartbreak Hotel" and a chair that was owned by Vincent van Gogh. Alice Cooper gave Paul a bed that once belonged to Groucho Marx.

The Beatles sometimes had their problems getting along. But even after they split up, they

"I still love those guys. The Beatles are over, but John, Paul, George and Ringo go on."
—John Lennon

played on each other's albums, and wrote songs and appeared onstage together. Ringo's song "Never Without You" was a tribute to George. Paul's "Here Today" was a tribute to John. George's "When We Was Fab" was about the Beatles.

Get Back to Where You Once Belonged

As soon as the Beatles broke up, there were rumors about a Beatles reunion. In 1976, they were offered *fifty million dollars* to do one show. They said no.

That same year, as a joke, *Saturday Night Live* offered the Beatles three thousand dollars if they'd come on the show and sing three songs. As it turned out, John and Paul were in New York that night, watching at John's apartment. They thought about going over to *SNL*. "We nearly got into a cab," John said. "But we were actually too tired." That was the last time John and Paul saw each other.

Nothing Is Real

The Beatles never did have a reunion, but they still play concerts. There are Beatles cover bands all over the world.

In 1977 *Beatlemania* was a Broadway musical with four Beatles look-alikes singing their songs. It was advertised as "Not the Beatles, but an incredible simulation." The show ran for two years until it was shut down by a lawsuit . . . from the Beatles!

Paul and Ringo gave their blessing to *The Beatles Love*, a Cirque du Soleil show that's been running in Las Vegas since 2006.

If you want to see something *like* the Beatles, watch the hilarious movie *The Rutles*. This Beatles parody band sings silly songs like "All You Need Is Cash" and "Can't Buy Me Lunch."

Actually, the Beatles *did* have one reunion, in a way. After John died, Yoko gave Paul tapes of songs John never finished. Paul, George, and Ringo worked on them and released two songs, "Free as a Bird" and "Real Love." They were the last real Beatles songs.

All the Children Sing

All four Beatles had children who became musicians. Ringo's son Zak Starkey was a drummer with the Who for many years.

John's sons Julian and Sean are singers. In 1984 Julian had a hit, "Too Late for Goodbyes." He also played drums on his dad's *Walls and Bridges* album.

George's son Dhani is a singer-songwriter whose band has appeared at Lollapalooza and Coachella.

Paul's son James played guitar and drums on his dad's albums, and he's also released two of his own.

But perhaps the most successful Beatle kid is Paul's daughter Stella McCartney. She's a world-famous fashion designer of clothing, jewelry, and cosmetics.

CHAPTER 12

Oh Yeah? (Stuff About the Beatles That Didn't Fit Anywhere Else)

What else have you got, Paige?

"Ringo" means "apple" in Japanese.

That's it?

No. There's a crater on Mercury named after John. An asteroid was named after Paul. And a planet was named after George.

When the Beatles toured America, parts of it were still segregated. When they were told black and white fans couldn't sit together at the Gator Bowl in Florida, the Beatles refused to appear. "We never play to segregated audiences," John said, "and we aren't going to start now."

All four Beatles were born while World War II was going on. Liverpool is a shipping port, so it was a target for Nazi bombing. Right near Ringo's house, a bomb killed three of his neighbors.

"We played on bomb sites a lot and I grew up thinking the word *bomb site* almost meant 'playground.'"
—Paul McCartney

The Beatles had twelve number one singles in a row, but thirteen was unlucky. "Strawberry Fields Forever/Penny Lane" only reached number two on the charts. The song that prevented it from being number one? "Release Me" by Engelbert Humperdinck.

Ho Ho Ho Hee Hee Hee Ha Ha Ha!

"We can laugh at anything—ourselves included."
—John Lennon

One thing that set the Beatles apart from other bands was that they were *funny*. During interviews, press conferences, and even concerts, they were constantly making wisecracks.

Some of their songs were jokes in themselves. "Eight Days a Week"? There are only seven days in a week! "Drive My Car"? It's about a guy who hires a driver but doesn't have a car!

During the Royal Command Performance before the Queen, John announced, "For our last number, I'd like to ask your help. Will the people in the cheaper seats, clap your hands. And the rest of you, if you'd just rattle your jewelry."

During a press conference, George was asked what the Beatles do when they're cooped up in hotel rooms. He replied, "We ice-skate."

John was asked, "How did you find America?" He replied, "Turn left at Greenland."

After John and Paul realized how much money they could earn by writing their own

"Everyone in Liverpool thinks they're a comedian."
—George Harrison

songs, they would get together for a songwriting session and say, "Let's write a swimming pool."

After their last public appearance, John said, "I'd like to say thank you on behalf of the group and ourselves and I hope we passed the audition."

The day John and Paul met, a guy named Bob Molyneux recorded some of the Quarry Men show on his tape recorder. For thirty-seven years, Molyneux didn't do anything with the tape. In 1994, he sold it for almost $200,000. The buyer? EMI, the Beatles' record company.

For Christmas one year, Brian Epstein gave each of the Beatles an alarm clock. They were often late for appointments, so he thought the clocks would help them be on time.

The Beatles were not great athletes. But there was one sport they *did* enjoy—bowling! The British loved American stuff, and bowling

became a craze there in 1961. Bowling alleys
stayed open late at night, so the Beatles would
hang out and bowl after they finished a show.

When the Beatles performed at Shea Stadium in
New York, Ringo's future wife Barbara and Paul's
future wife Linda were in the audience.

The Beatles didn't invent music videos, but they
were video pioneers. When they stopped touring,
they needed a way to spread the word about their
new songs. Instead of doing lots of TV
appearances, they made video clips that could be
shown over and over. You can watch those early
videos on YouTube: "Paperback Writer," "Rain,"
"Day Tripper," "Help!," "Ticket to Ride," "I Feel
Fine," and "We Can Work It Out."

The Cavern, where the Beatles got their start, was demolished in 1973 and turned into a parking lot. A new Cavern was built using bricks from the original club.

The last Beatles concert was at Candlestick Park in San Francisco in 1966. Almost fifty years later, the stadium was torn down. The final concert—Paul McCartney.

Might Win an Oscar,
You Can Never Tell

Besides *A Hard Day's Night* and *Help!* The Beatles were involved in lots of movies. John acted in *How I Won the War*. Ringo was in *The Magic Christian*. George started HandMade Films, which produced movies such as *Monty Python's Life of Brian*.

Beatles songs have been in lots of movies—*The Social Network*, *Ferris Bueller's Day Off*, *Jojo Rabbit*, *The Boss Baby*, *Minions*, and *Superman III*.

No one knows why, but the movie *Help!* is dedicated to Elias Howe, the guy who invented the sewing machine.

How will we find Mordor?

Turn left at Greenland.

There was one Beatles movie that never happened.

In 1968 there was a plan for them to star in
J. R. R. Tolkien's *Lord of the Rings*.

The Rolling Stones vs.
the Beatles

The two bands were considered to be rivals,
and fans would pledge their loyalty to one or
the other. But actually, the Beatles and the
Stones were friends. In fact, George helped the
Stones get their first record contract.

After John and Paul wrote "I Wanna Be Your
Man," they gave it to the Stones. It became their
first hit. That was the only song recorded by
both groups.

On the cover of *Sgt. Pepper* is a doll wearing
a sweater that says WELCOME THE ROLLING STONES
on the front and GOOD GUYS on the sleeve.
Six months later the Stones album *Their
Satanic Majesties Request* came out, with the
faces of the four Beatles hidden on it.

Can't Get No Worse

Not everything the Beatles did was successful. They made a TV movie of *Magical Mystery Tour* that got poor ratings and most people agreed it was bad.

They opened a clothing store in London called Apple Boutique. Eight months later, they closed it and gave all the clothes away.

At one point the Beatles decided to buy some private islands near Greece so they could live there and make music away from screaming fans. After visiting the islands, they decided it was a dumb idea.

Let's end this section with the worst Beatles song ever. I vote for "Mr. Moonlight."

Yeah, that's terrible. But I vote for "You Know My Name (Look Up the Number)." It's *horrible*.

How do we decide which was worse?

Wait, I changed my mind. The worst Beatles song has to be "Revolution 9."

Oh yeah. I agree. Was that even a song?

Who knows? It's unlistenable. I guess that just proves nobody's perfect.

The Songs Are Mine

In 1981 Paul teamed up with Michael Jackson on songs such as "The Girl Is Mine." Michael didn't know much about the music business back then, and Paul told him how he could make a lot of money by buying the rights to other people's music. Paul owned twenty-five thousand songs, including Buddy Holly's songs and the Broadway musicals *Guys & Dolls*, *The Music Man*, *Grease*, *A Chorus Line*, and *Annie*. So you know what Michael did?

He bought the rights to the Beatles' music!

129

Yes! After *Thriller* became a hit, Michael spent forty-seven *million* dollars to buy the Beatles' song catalog. Paul was *not* happy. After MJ died in 2009, Paul bought back some of the songs.

Their record company didn't think Beatles records would sell in Germany unless they were sung in German. So the Beatles re-recorded the vocals for "She Loves You" ("Sie Liebt Dich") and "I Want To Hold Your Hand" ("Komm, Gib Mir Deine Hand").

Steve Jobs was a big Beatles fan. He named Apple Computer after the Beatles' record company. The Beatles sued, and Apple Computer was only allowed to use the word "Apple" if its products had nothing to do with music.

Yeah, then iTunes and iPods came along. The Beatles sued again, and Apple had to pay them twenty-six million dollars.

Well, that's it. I can see the back cover from here. The book is finished! Just think—at this very moment, there might be two teenagers like John and Paul meeting for the first time, and someday they may change the world. Isn't that cool?

Hold on! You never told me your favorite Beatles song!

"Wait"

I've *been* waiting!

"I'm So Tired"

Do you want to lie down?

"I Feel Fine"

Good. So what's your favorite Beatles song?

"Think for Yourself"

But I'm asking you.

"Your Mother Should Know"

What does Mom have to do with it?

"She's a Woman"

So what? Look, this is a simple question. Just name your favorite Beatles song.

"Help!"

AND IN THE END THE LOVE YOU TAKE IS EQUAL TO the love you make

—the Beatles

TO FIND OUT MORE . . .

Did we get you interested in the Beatles? Yay! If you want to find out more, there are thousands of books, videos, and websites. And of course, you can listen to their music.

ACKNOWLEDGMENTS

Thanks to Kristin Allard, Peter Blau, Simon Boughton, Dave Cole, Ray Dimetrosky, Steven DiPilla, Sandy Ressler, Andrew Ross, Jackie Spencer, Allison Steinfeld, Stephen Swinburne, Liza Voges, and Nina Wallace.

The information in this book came from many sources. Especially helpful was Mark Lewisohn's *Tune In: The Beatles: All These Years*, William J. Dowlding's *Beatlesongs*, Steve Turner's *A Hard Day's Write*, *The Lyrics* by Paul McCartney, *The Beatles Anthology*, and *The Beatles Bible*.

ABOUT THE AUTHOR

Dan Gutman's life changed when he saw the Beatles on *The Ed Sullivan Show* when he was nine years old. Dan has since written many books for young readers, such as the My Weird School series, the Genius Files series, the Flashback Four series, *Houdini and Me*, *The Kid Who Ran for President*, *The Homework Machine*, and his baseball card adventure books. Dan and his wife, Nina, live in New York City. You can find out more about Dan and his books by visiting his website (www.dangutman.com) or following him on Facebook, Twitter, and Instagram.

TITLES IN THE
Wait! WHAT?
SERIES